PLANTS
to the
RESCUE!

NEON 🦑 SQUID

CONTENTS

READY TO DIG INTO THE WORLD OF PLANTS?

Hi there, new friends! My name is Vikram Baliga, and I'm so excited to meet you. Before we dive into this book, I want to introduce myself a little. I have a PhD in horticulture (which mostly just means I've studied plants for a LONG time) and spend my days teaching college students about plants, as well as managing a garden and a greenhouse. I have a son named Bradley and a wonderful wife named Alana. I grew up gardening with my granddad and have loved plants my whole life.

This book is a look at how amazing and complex plants are, and in particular all of the ways they're helping us face tricky challenges—from how to produce enough food to dealing with climate change. It's intended to give you a glimpse into the incredible work that plant scientists are doing all around the world and show you why there is so much hope for our future. I can't wait to take you on this journey through the world of plants and show you all the ways plants are coming to our rescue!

VIKRAM BALIGA

That's me!

THE CHALLENGES

Our world is changing quickly! Over the past few hundred years, humans have done things to make it change even faster. While we've come up with some pretty cool stuff (such as cars and planes), we've unfortunately also harmed the environment, making life harder for ourselves and the plants and animals that share the Earth with us.

Some energy escapes into space.

Light energy (heat) comes from the sun.

Some energy is trapped by Earth's atmosphere, heating the planet.

CLIMATE CHANGE
Climate change is the long-term shift in weather patterns and global temperatures. While this is generally a natural process, human activity since the 1800s has made it happen a lot faster. We started making things in factories on a grand scale. To do this we needed to burn fossil fuels, which have caused our atmosphere to change and trap heat. This is called the greenhouse effect. As a result the planet is getter warmer and weirder.

WHAT ARE FOSSIL FUELS?
Fossil fuels—such as coal, oil, and natural gas—come from decomposing plants and animals that died a *long* time ago. They're found in the Earth's crust and can be burned for energy to run our cars and heat our homes. They're really useful, but they can harm the environment and make climate change worse.

POLLUTION

Pollution comes from us putting things into the environment that aren't supposed to be there—including trash, harmful chemicals, and greenhouse gases (gases from burning fossil fuels that trap heat in the atmosphere). Pollution harms wildlife, damages ecosystems, and speeds up climate change.

EXTREME WEATHER

The weather isn't just getting hotter, it's getting more extreme. Higher temperatures mess with weather patterns, making things more dangerous. We're now seeing stronger tornadoes and hurricanes, bigger wildfires, and longer droughts.

EXPANDING POPULATIONS

The world population is expected to reach almost 10 billion by 2050. That's a lot of people! We need to figure out how to make sure we have all the resources we need while also protecting the environment.

LOSS OF HABITAT

Animals need places to live and food to eat. While many of them build their own homes, others use trees, dense shrubs, or other plants for food and shelter. Deforestation (cutting down forests), urbanization (building bigger cities), and climate change are all destroying habitats, making it harder for animals to survive.

BEATING THE HEAT

Humans are pretty smart, but beating climate change and saving the world is a big task. Luckily for us, we're not alone in this fight. Plants have been adapting to changes on this planet for millions of years. They're really good at it and are coming to our rescue! As plants continue to deal with hotter summers and more extreme weather, they can give our scientists lots of little (and some really big) clues about how we can do the same.

ADJUSTING TO CHANGE

Some common crops, such as tomatoes and eggplants, struggle to produce fruit in really hot weather. But they have a wild cousin—silverleaf nightshade—that can withstand temperatures of nearly 140°F (60°C) and keep flowering and fruiting. Scientists are working to breed this super tough plant with tomatoes and eggplants (peppers, too) in the hope of creating more resilient crops. It just shows, the answers to our problems can often be found in nature...

Silverleaf
nightshade

WHAT IS A PLANT?

You probably have an idea of what a plant is in your mind, but what exactly makes them so special? Most plants have leaves, stems, and roots, and they're an important source of food for animals and humans. Plants produce their own food through a process called photosynthesis, in which they turn light from the sun, water from the soil, and carbon dioxide (CO_2) from the air into the sugars they need to grow.

SUNLIGHT
Light from the sun contains lots of energy. Plants capture the energy using a special green pigment in their leaves called chlorophyll. They use the energy to turn carbon into sugar.

CARBON DIOXIDE
Remember greenhouse gases? CO_2 (made of carbon and oxygen) is one of them. While we breathe it out, plants take in CO_2 and use the carbon to create sugars.

WATER
Plants move water from the soil, through their stems, and into the air (in the form of water vapor). This process is called transpiration.

ROOTS AND SOIL
Soil is super important for healthy plants! It contains the water and nutrients they need to grow. As roots get bigger and search through the soil, they're able to give their plants a drink and anchor them to the ground.

OXYGEN

Oxygen is a pretty big deal. Most organisms on the planet need oxygen to survive, and plants make it for us. After they snag the carbon from CO_2 they release the leftover oxygen into the air. Thanks, plants!

TYPES OF PLANTS

Plants come in all shapes and sizes, just like people! They all have features that help them adapt to different conditions and perform specific jobs in their environments. Below are a few of the terms we use to describe plants.

Monocots have grasslike leaves.

Dicots have broad leaves.

Perennials live for many years.

Annuals live for one year.

POLLINATION

Pollination is part of the process plants use to reproduce (create more plants). Insects and other pollinators carry pollen from flower to flower—and get a free meal in the process. This produces seeds that grow into new plants.

Angiosperms have flowers and fruits.

Gymnosperms have cones and needles.

Bulb plants survive winters underground.

Wildflowers grow from seeds.

FILLING OUR PLATES

RICE
The most widely consumed crop in the world, rice feeds billions of people every day. It's typically grown in really wet conditions, often in flooded fields called paddies. Scientists are working hard to try to make rice easier to grow in more climates.

RICE WORK
Dr. Norman Borlaug's work in creating new kinds of rice and wheat is thought to have saved nearly 100 million lives around the world! He developed wheat plants that produced four times more grain than usual and had shorter, stronger stems that could handle all of the extra weight.

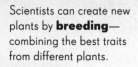

Scientists can create new plants by **breeding**—combining the best traits from different plants.

Figuring out how to feed all the hungry people in the world is going to be one of the biggest challenges we've ever faced. While plants are amazing sources of food, scientists are figuring out how to make sure we're growing them as efficiently as possible.

Combine harvester

WHEAT

Wheat is another popular crop worldwide, nourishing people through baked goods, cereals, drinks, and more. Wheat is usually harvested (picked) using combine harvesters, tractors, and other machines. This means the plants have to all be the same size and height to make them easier to pick.

Wheat plants used to have long stems and small amounts of grain.

Norman's new and improved crop!

NOT EVERYONE'S A FAN

Some methods of plant breeding are controversial. Genetically modified plants are created in a lab using cutting-edge science. This technology has already done a lot of good, but it's new and some people don't trust it.

BANANA

Wherever you live in the world, there's a good chance you've eaten a banana before. But did you know that bananas don't just make tasty snacks? A banana plant is pretty huge, and the fruit itself is pretty small, so people have come up with clever ways to use the rest of the plant!

A banana plant is actually a type of herb.

NICE HAIRDO

Fiber from the trunks of banana trees can be used to create hair extensions, or fake hair that can be glued or clipped to your hair to change your style. Using bananas instead of plastic extensions reduces waste and can help prevent the itchiness that some hair extensions cause. Win-win!

FOOD PACKAGING

Scientists in Australia have found a way to turn the trunks of banana trees into a special kind of film that could be used as food packaging. This could be used as an eco-friendly alternative to plastic. Banana leaves can also be steamed and then used to wrap up packed lunches!

DR. BANANA

It turns out that banana peels are not just for slipping on. They can be used to treat sunburn, bug bites, and minor scrapes. The peel contains special anti-inflammatory properties!

SHINY SHOES

Don't ask us who first came up with this idea, but it turns out that rubbing banana peel on leather shoes can make them shine! This trick means avoiding the chemicals used in traditional shoe polish. Your shoes might smell a little like bananas though...

OUR FRIEND, ALGAE

Algae isn't exactly a plant, but it does a lot of plantlike things, so I've decided it's OK to include in this book. Most importantly, it photosynthesizes, turning sunlight and carbon dioxide into sugar and releasing oxygen into the atmosphere. From being a food source for animals to a fuel for our cars, algae has the potential to be a solution for many of our problems.

CLEANER FUEL?

Burning fossil fuels (see page 6) provides us with energy, but it unfortunately also causes pollution. Fossil fuels also take thousands of years to make. Luckily this is where our friend algae comes in. But what exactly is algae?

PLANTLIKE

Algae are actually a number of different organisms that lack roots, stems, leaves, and other things that plants normally have. They often live in large colonies, like the green stuff you see floating on ponds, but they can resemble plants—for example, seaweed and kelp.

Organisms in the ocean, including algae, produce more than 50% of the oxygen on Earth!

One day all of
our cars could be
powered by biofuels.

FUELS OF THE FUTURE

Unlike fossil fuels, biofuels are renewable, can be made quickly from plants and algae, and create *way* less pollution. Most of the biofuels we use today come from crops like corn, sugarcane, and soybeans. These work well, but they require a lot of space to grow. Algae can be easily grown and harvested in smaller spaces and may be the next big thing in biofuel technology!

ALGAE MACHINES

Bioreactors are big machines that can be filled with algae and harness their special abilities. Algae in bioreactors can be used to turn sunlight into energy, trap and store carbon dioxide, filter air, clean water, or create biofuels. Scientists are really interested in biofuels, because they have some serious advantages over fossil fuels.

FARMER'S FRIEND

Fertilizers are used to help plants grow. Human-made fertilizers can be expensive to make and can cause lots of problems for the planet. Algae, however, can be used instead. As algae decomposes, it leaves behind the nutrients plants need to grow.

SUPER SEEDS

From tiny daisies to giant redwood trees, most plants begin their life cycle as a seed. Seeds are the result of pollination—pollen being taken from one flower to another. They are produced by plants and are often contained in cones (such as a pine cone) or fruits (such as an apple). Seeds are the key to the future of plants, so scientists are working on creating super seeds that will be able to help us in the years to come.

GROWING A PLANT

So much technology and science goes into developing new kinds of seeds, but the process of growing a plant is pretty much the same whether you're doing it in a lab or a pot on your kitchen table. Let's take a quick look at how it works!

1. Grab some soil and plant your seed in a small hole.

2. Water is the first thing a seed needs—give it plenty!

3. A seed will **germinate** (a seedling will appear) in a few days.

4. Soon you'll have a plant, ready to make its own seeds!

MAKING BETTER SEEDS

Seeds tend to grow plants with traits most likely to help them survive... eventually. This is called natural selection, and it takes a long time. But sometimes we need better seeds in a hurry! Scientists are constantly working to come up with seeds that will do better in a changing environment.

Diseases are always on the prowl. Scientists can give seeds specific qualities to help fight them off.

SEED VAULTS

Seeds are all different as they take **genes** from both parent plants to make something new. Sometimes scientists find helpful qualities or traits in seeds that they want to keep. These seeds are kept under lock and key in special seed vaults underground—ready to be brought out if we ever need their specific qualities.

We can't just throw a winter coat and mittens on our plants, so scientists need to breed special seeds that can cope with extreme cold.

The world is getting hotter and drier. Seeds that can grow well in high temperatures with limited water are going to be important.

Bugs think seeds are an easy snack. Creating seeds with special anti-bug coatings can help baby plants survive.

SPINACH EMAILS

Spinach roots are very sensitive to their environment.

Scientists at the Massachusetts Institute of Technology (MIT) have created spinach that can send emails. You read that right. This, of course, leads us to two important questions: How? And why?! The answers are all to do with a spinach plant's roots...

THE ROOT OF THE PROBLEM

Spinach plants grow big root systems. These roots spend their time exploring the soil, looking for water and nutrients to help them grow. Turns out, they can find many other things that can teach us more about their environment too! From microorganisms to harmful chemicals, spinach roots can provide us with lots of information.

NANOTUBES

To make the most of the information spinach roots can provide, scientists had to figure out a way of getting technology INSIDE spinach plants. And the way they did it was by implanting tiny carbon nanotubes inside their leaves.

Nanotechnology is the science of really tiny things.

YOU'VE GOT MAIL

When the spinach plants pull up water with toxins or other harmful chemicals dissolved in it, the tubes send signals to a monitor that emails the information back to the scientists. This technology could be used to record changes in the soil, warning us about pollution, climate change, and other problems. At this moment in time the technology isn't being used in the real world, but give it time...

SPINACH: Something you should see here, guys!

SCIENTISTS: Nice work, Agent Spinach!

From: Spinach
"Pollution detected"

From: Spinach
"All clear today"

From: Spinach
"Worm problems"

From: Cabbage
"We need to talk"

POWER PLANTS

We use power for almost everything we do in today's world. There's a good chance you're using some right now to light up a bulb so you can read this book! The problem is that lots of the methods we use to create power at the moment harm the environment. But what if we could get our power directly from plants that are already harvesting energy from the sun? It could change everything!

CAPTURING ELECTRICITY

The relationship between plants, soil, and the little critters that live in the soil is complicated. As **microorganisms** feed on roots and decaying plant material, they release electricity. This electricity could be harvested by special electrodes attached to plant roots or buried nearby in the soil.

THE NEXT STEP

Plants have long been used as one of our main power sources. Most fossil fuels come from decomposed plants, not dinosaurs. Biofuels come from corn and other crops. We burn wood for energy and heat. As we try to find new ways to reduce pollution and fight climate change, using living plants to power our cars and homes will be even more important.

SOLAR PANELS

You've probably seen solar panels sitting on someone's roof, soaking up the sun's rays and turning them into electricity. It's cool technology, but plants have been doing the same thing for millions of years. Scientists are working on ways to capture some of the leftover energy from plant photosynthesis. If they could do that, we could power our homes with the plants in our gardens!

WIND POWER

Right now, most wind power comes from giant windmills that generate electricity as they spin. That's not the only way though... Wires could be attached to branches and trunks, producing power as trees and other plants naturally move with the wind.

FUNKY FUNGI

OK, OK, I know that fungi aren't technically plants—but they serve many of the same roles in the environment and they don't look like animals, so they often get lumped together! They're plant-ish and do SO MANY cool things, so mycologists (fungus scientists) and plant scientists are working together to find amazing new ways to use fungi.

MUSHROOM BURGERS

Mushrooms are the fruiting parts of some fungi. Do you like mushrooms on your pizza? Food scientists and researchers are looking into new types of food that can be made from them. Mushrooms contain lots of fiber and protein and make a great meat substitute for people trying to live plant-based lives—mushroom burger, anyone? Some fungi can even be powdered and added to coffee to wake up sleepy adults in the morning!

FERTILIZERS

Like our algae friends, decomposing fungi contain lots of nutrients and can be used as eco-friendly fertilizers. Adding these fertilizers to crops will help them grow more strongly.

MUSHROOM BRICKS

What if we could grow buildings? Agricultural waste, such as straw and corn husks, can be mixed with fungi in a brick-shaped mold, grown for a couple of weeks, then heated. The resulting bricks are amazingly strong and durable, and they can be grown into any shape you can think of!

FAKE LEATHER

Many people are choosing to stay away from animal products, such as leather, and are looking for plant-based, sustainable options. A company has found a way to grow mycelium (sort of like fungus roots) into a material that looks and feels just like leather. It can be made into belts, shoes, and jackets.

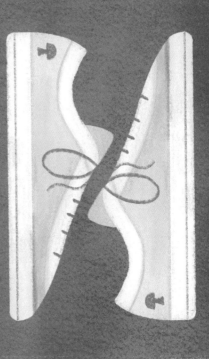

NEW MEDICINE

Penicillin, an antibiotic developed from a type of bread mold in the early 1900s, has changed the world and saved millions of lives. Today, different species of fungi are being investigated to see if they can be used to create medicine to treat all sorts of diseases and infections. Some of these antibiotics could even be used to make organ transplants easier.

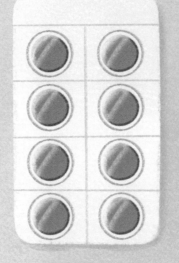

PACKAGING

Plastic packaging leads to as much waste and pollution as almost anything else we use. Fungi can be used to create strong, compostable packaging.

THE CLEAN-UP CREW

Some of the most devastating events we see on the news are oil spills. Whether from a sinking ship or a burst well, oil and petroleum products can hurt wildlife and cause long-term damage to the environment. Ecologists use a range of different tools to try to get rid of oil, but fungi may hold the secrets that will help us get the job done!

DEVASTATING IMPACT

Wildlife and oil do not mix. If animals accidentally eat oil it makes them sick, and it can hurt their eyes. It also makes it hard for them to walk, fly, or swim if they get covered in the sticky stuff. Oil is also hydrophobic (which means it repels water) so it's really hard for biologists to wash it off our animal friends! Plants and coral are also at risk from oil spills.

HUNGRY MUSHROOMS

Oyster mushrooms have shown an amazing ability to eat petroleum, which may make them the prime candidate for dealing with oil spills. It's possible that scientists could create mats covered in these fungi that would float out in the ocean or be placed on a beach and help clean up after a spill.

Some fungi can use oil as a source of **food** and quickly drink it up!

LOOK OUT, PLASTIC!

Plastics, from milk bottles to the pots we grow our plants in, break down *super* slowly in landfills. They are one of the biggest sources of trash and pollution in the world. Fungi can help us with this problem, too! Scientists have discovered that some kinds of fungi can consume plastic waste, safely recycling it back into the ecosystem.

GLOW IN THE DARK

We've all used bedside lamps and nightlights, but what if you could be reading this book by plantlight? Scientists have discovered they can make plants glow in the dark!

HOW IT WORKS

To make a plant glow, scientists inject its leaves with nanoparticles that can absorb light energy and release it slowly at night. In the future, genes from glowing animals could be added to plants so they would be able to naturally glow. What a bright idea!

Scientists have managed to make watercress glow...

...as well as basil!

WHAT'S THE POINT?

Glowing plants may sound silly, but they could have a huge impact. Electric lights use a lot of energy, and they can mess with animals that navigate by starlight or use the dark to hunt. Imagine roads lined with glowing trees, bright enough to see where you're going but soft enough to be wildlife friendly. Also, how cool would it be if your favorite houseplant was also your lamp?!

GLOWING IN NATURE

Plenty of things in nature already glow. This is called **bioluminescence** and it is caused by chemical reactions. Deep sea squid and anglerfish use their ability to glow to hunt in the dark, while fireflies light themselves up to attract mates. By studying these animals, scientists have a better idea of how to make plants glow.

Scientists from the Massachusetts Institute of Technology made plants that glow for more than an hour!

CACTUS BAGS

Plastic bags are handy for us and cheap to produce, but they are a scourge on the environment. Thinking about throwing away a plastic bag? Think again—they take up to 1,000 years to decompose! Plastic bags are also dangerous for marine animals. Fish get tangled in them, and sea turtles mistake them for jellyfish and eat them. Luckily, scientists in Mexico, led by Sandra Pascoe Ortiz, have realized they can make plastic-bag replacements using prickly cacti. They do this in a few simple steps.

2 EXTRACT THE JUICE
Next the cactus strips are passed through a processor, which squeezes them to produce cactus juice.

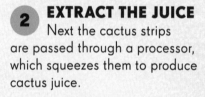

1 CUT THE CATCUS
Scientists cut and peel a prickly pear cactus leaf. These plants grow in the wild in Mexico.

3 ADD A SPECIAL FORMULA
After the juice has been refrigerated, a special nontoxic formula is added.

4 ROLL IT OUT
The scientists pour the juice on a flat surface, roll it out, and let it dry.

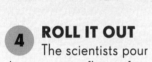

5 TA-DA!
Eventually the cactus juice will turn into a sticky, bendy substance that can be shaped into bags, or even cutlery!

MAKING NEW PLANTS

One of our big challenges as we come up with exciting new features in plants is to make sure they stick around! Cross-pollination (pollen moving from one plant to another) leads to new varieties of plants being created all the time. Sometimes this means we lose important qualities in a plant. To combat this, scientists are coming up with ways to clone plants and keep the traits we want.

THE CLONES

The simplest way to clone plants is to take cuttings from them. If you snip off a section from one plant and then put it in soil, it will start to grow roots. It can take a while and is tougher with some species, but once you figure out the details you can create a clone of the original plant!

AMAZING CELLS

Every living thing is made up of tiny units called **cells**. Incredibly, every single plant cell contains all of the information necessary to be any type of plant cell. For example, a leaf cell can turn into a root cell. Scientists in a lab can take advantage of this and grow entire new plants from just a few leaf cells.

FRUIT SALAD TREE
Multiple varieties of the same (or similar) kinds of fruit can all be grafted together onto the same tree! How cool would it be to have a tree in your garden growing different kinds of fruit?

GRAFTING

Grafting is the process of taking buds or branches from one plant and attaching them to another, closely related plant. We do this to combine the best traits from different species. For example, a peach tree that has great fruit could be grafted to another peach tree with super strong roots to get the best of both worlds!

To graft two plants you take a section of one plant and insert it into the stem of another.

Then you tape up the joined section to protect it until it has grafted together.

ALOE VERA

Native to Africa and the Arabian Peninsula, there are dozens of species of aloe vera, many of which are popular house plants. In addition to adding some greenery to your home, aloe has served many purposes throughout history.

ANCIENT EGYPTIANS

The ancient Egyptians were some of the first people to realize how amazing aloe vera is. They called it the "plant of immortality" because it could grow and flower in harsh conditions, sometimes even without soil. They discovered many of its medicinal properties and sometimes buried it with dead royals as an offering to the gods.

WHAT A COOL PLANT

Sunburn is no fun at all. Fortunately, treating sunburn is one of aloe vera's specialties! The gel in its leaves causes a cooling effect on the skin, providing pain relief, and has been shown to speed healing. It can also be used to treat minor cuts and scapes, mosquito bites, and bacterial infections.

AT THE PHARMACY

Aloe vera has been used in different cosmetics for thousands of years. Today, it's in everything from lotions and sunscreens to hair-care products, such as shampoo and conditioner. Research is also starting to show that aloe vera may be helpful in fighting acne and other skin problems.

MEDICINE

Aloe vera can also be made into medicine. Research has shown that aloe vera–based medicines may regulate blood sugar, aid digestion, and reduce stress.

SAVE OUR SOIL!

Soil is so much more than the dirt that gets stuck in your shoes. Made of sand, silt, and clay, a healthy soil is one of the most important things for plants and ecosystems. Soil is where plants get their water, nutrients, and support. In return, plants help take care of the soil. Scientists are working on finding ways to make sure that soils all over the world stay healthy.

45% solids

5% organic matter

50% space

THE DUST BOWL

If you ever want an example of how important soil is, just look at the Dust Bowl in the United States in the 1930s to 1940s. Partly due to bad soil management, this period saw extreme droughts and ruined harvests. When soil isn't taken care of, it can blow away in giant dust clouds.

SURFACE MULCHING

As any good gardener knows, mulching leads to happy plants. A **mulch** is anything, including leaves, shredded wood, and bark, that covers up the surface of the soil. As these things break down they add nutrients to the soil. A few inches of mulch keeps the soil cooler, retains moisture for thirsty plants, and helps prevent weeds!

PERFECT SOIL

The ideal soil is made up of 50% space (containing either air or water), 45% solids (sand, silt, and clay), and 5% organic mater, which mostly comes from decaying plants.

JUICY ROOTS

Plant roots explore the soil looking for air, nutrients, and water. And when they die, they add nutrients to the soil. Plants with strong root systems can make channels for water to move through and help protect the soil from blowing away. Plants of the future could be specially bred to help support and improve poor quality soil.

CAREFUL PLANTING

How and where you plant your plants is important. Digging the soil and planting the same crops year after year have been common farming practices for a long time, but scientists have found that this can destroy soil over time. Instead, reducing digging and rotating where you put plant species protects and builds up the soil.

NO SOIL, NO PROBLEM

As our population increases, we're looking for new ways and new places to grow food. Hydroponics and aeroponics are two exciting methods for growing plants without soil!

HYDROPONICS

Hydroponics has actually been used for thousands of years, but now we're using it in new and clever ways. Named from the Greek words for "water" (*hydro*) and "to work" (*ponos*), it's a practice where plants are grown just by using water that contains lots of useful **nutrients**. Some hydroponic systems are like big tanks containing plants on floating rafts, while others constantly circulate water through pipes or trays.

THE FUTURE OF GROWING?

The coolest thing about hydroponic and aeroponic systems is they can be built and run almost anywhere—from old, abandoned shopping centers to the outsides of skyscrapers. These methods could be a total game changer for providing enough food for people to eat in big cities.

AEROPONICS

Aeroponics is another technique that doesn't require soil and can be done almost anywhere. Unlike hydroponics, which has plant roots grown in the water, these systems suspend plants in the air. High-pressure nozzles spray mist onto the hanging roots to keep them wet and supplied with the nutrients they need to grow. Maybe one day in the future you'll have Brussel sprouts hanging from your kitchen ceiling!

PLANTS IN SPACE

As humans continue to explore the solar system, scientists are trying to figure out how to grow plants in space. After all, if we one day set up bases on the moon or Mars, astronauts are going to need food to eat! While there are some challenges—plants are pretty attached to *our* planet after all—researchers have come up with a few ideas for how we could grow tomatoes or potatoes on a different world.

MARTIAN GREENHOUSES

Mars is a dead planet without breathable air or healthy soil. To grow plants on Mars we'd need to make special greenhouses that would be sealed up, filled with an Earthlike atmosphere, and fitted with beds full of the soil and bacteria plants recognize. Technology like hydroponics and aeroponics could eliminate the need for soil entirely. Plants could also be installed in brightly lit, rotating chambers to simulate the sunlight and gravity we have on Earth, so they know which direction to grow in. Imagine being a farmer on Mars!

Astronauts in space have successfully grown bok choy they can eat!

A rotating greenhouse could simulate Earth's gravity.

ASTRONAUT FARMERS

We don't need to wait until we reach Mars to try out some of these growing techniques. The International Space Station is home to cutting-edge research on a wide variety of plants. Astronauts in the station care for and study these plants to see how they respond to low-gravity conditions and life in space. Figuring out which plants cope best will help us in the future.

MAKE IT RAIN

Rainfall is one of the main ways fresh water gets into lakes, streams, and gardens. Eventually this rain makes its way into your glass so you can drink it. But did you know plants play a crucial role in creating rainfall? They've been helping the process for millions of years! With increasing drought across the planet, planting more plants and trees in the right places may help provide more rain.

CLOUD CREATORS

As we learned earlier in this book, plants get water from the soil. The plants move the water through their roots and stems to their leaves, before releasing it into the atmosphere in the form of water vapor, which is a type of gas. This process increases the amount of moisture in the air. Eventually this moisture turns into clouds!

THE WATER CYCLE

All the water on our planet has been here all along. It's never "used up." It just changes form and moves from place to place. Energy from the sun heats water on the ground, turning it into water vapor. This process is called **evaporation**. This water vapor combines with that released by plants, turns into clouds, then condenses into rain, which hits the ground and starts the cycle again.

Water vapor exits plants through openings on the leaves called stomata.

The process of plants moving water into the atmosphere is called transpiration.

COULD WE HELP?

Some people have wondered if we could give clouds a helping hand to make them rain. Experiments over time have tried to put different types of particles in clouds to help water vapor fall as rain (this process is called **condensation**). It can be effective on a small scale, but it is not a long-term solution. Plants and trees are a better bet!

In experiments special particles have been dropped into clouds by planes.

CLEANING THE AIR

Pollution from cars, planes, and factories is constantly being pumped into the atmosphere. It's not great for people who like breathing fresh air! Pollution causes health problems, damages buildings and roads, and harms the environment. Luckily, plants have lots of tricks for removing pesky pollutants from the air.

OXYGEN GIVERS

Because of photosynthesis, all plants produce oxygen. (Even algae get in on the game.) This means that having healthy gardens and green spaces in our towns and cities and around our homes literally helps us breathe more easily!

SMOG

Smog is a word meaning "smoke fog" that was first used in the early 1900s. As coal was burned to power new industries, people realized that a toxic haze was constantly hanging in the air. Smog causes numerous health problems, but it's getting better! Laws passed around the world over the past 50 years have reduced smog and really cleaned up the air.

AIR FILTERS

Plant leaves make perfect air filters. Polluting particles in the air are caught by leaves and eventually drop to the soil, where they can be broken down by tiny living things called **microorganisms**. That's why it's a good idea to have trees planted around your yard. Plants with dense foliage, such as conifer trees, are especially good at trapping pollution.

CLEANING THE RAIN

Remember how trees can make it rain? When rain falls it collects polluting particles from the air and brings them to the ground. While this can lead to some problems, like acid rain, it also gives plants and soil the chance to trap those pollutants and filter the rain back into clean water.

PEACE AND QUIET

Noise pollution can be just as annoying as air pollution! If you've ever lived near a busy road, you know how distracting it can be. By putting trees and other plants between you and these roads, you can use the dense canopies to muffle sounds and let you live in peace.

BEWARE THE FERTILIZER

As long as we've been growing plants, we've been using some kind of **fertilizer** to make them grow better. We started by using manure (animal poop!) and compost, before creating artificial fertilizers in the 1940s. These fertilizers are very effective and let us grow way more crops, but are they good for the planet? Could plants offer a solution to this problem too?

DANGER TO THE OCEANS

If we use too much fertilizer on our fields, the plants and soils struggle to absorb all of it. The extra fertilizer runs into streams and rivers, and eventually lakes and oceans. This pollution can lead to "blooms," or very large colonies, of algae. Too much algae is not good! It can change the chemical balance of the water, hurting fish and other wildlife.

THE ROOT OF THE PROBLEM

It's not just human-made fertilizers that can help plants grow. Plants such as peas, beans, and peanuts work with fungi in the soil to absorb the gas nitrogen out of the air. As these plants and their roots decompose in the soil, the nitrogen is left behind and can help fertilize future generations of plants.

SUPER GEL

The plant world is providing many of the tools and new ideas we need to make the fertilizers of the future. Scientists have found a tropical kind of corn with a nifty ability. It has aerial roots (roots that don't go in soil) that can pull nitrogen out of the air and store it in a sticky gel. This gel surround the roots, acting as a fertilizer. This is rare and unique, but it may be able to be bred into other plants, allowing them to fertilize themselves.

Plants use aerial roots to climb things, catch water, and provide extra support.

Ponds collect rainwater and provide homes for lots of insects and amphibians.

NATURAL GROWING

What if we could grow food in a different way? Permaculture (short for "permanent agriculture") is not a new concept, but it has become more popular recently. The basic idea is that people try to recreate natural environments with lots of vegetables, flowers, and fruit trees that would have grown together in the wild. Year after year, the plants will continue to produce food and provide homes for lots of wildlife.

HELPFUL INSECTS

Permaculture aims to reduce the amount of **insecticides**—harmful chemicals used to try to get rid of pests. One way to accomplish this is to grow plants that will attract insects that you want to visit. For instance, if you have ladybugs in your garden, they will eat all of the aphids that could damage your plants.

Orchards of fruit trees provide shade, habitats for wildlife, and lots of food!

NO WASTE

Recyling, composting, and finding other ways to reduce waste is important to a good permaculture garden. Everything from old tree leaves to grass clippings to your tomato plants at the end of the growing season can find a new purpose. The compost you make from garden waste can then be used to give next year's plants a boost!

GARDENING ROBOTS

Technology could play a big role in future permaculture gardens. New robots are being developed that can identify weeds, recognize when plants need water or fertilizer, and find insect pests—before solving all of these problems for us!

BEET

Beet and its cousin sugar beet are incredible root vegetables used to make everything from medicines to table sugar. They have a unique, earthy flavor and add a lot of color to any dinner plate! Let's find out what makes these plants so special.

FOOD AND DRINK
Unlike plants where only some parts are edible, we can eat ALL of a beet. The leaves can be used fresh in a salad or cooked—often fried or steamed. The bright red roots can be roasted, boiled, steamed, or pickled. They can also be eaten raw or blended into a smoothie!

SUPERFOOD
Beet is one of the healthiest vegetables you can eat! It contains high levels of lots of things that are good for your body, including **nutrients**, fiber, and vitamin C. Eating or drinking beet has been shown to manage blood sugar and reduce blood pressure. Beet is one supercharged little veggie!

NATURAL DYES
Beets come in many colors, but they are usually a deep crimson red. Because of this, they're commonly used as a red (and sometimes yellow) dye for fabrics. Europeans in the 1800s used the juice from beets to dye their hair and create makeup!

SWEET BEETS
A plant called sugarcane is grown all over the world to make sugar, but it can take a lot of resources and needs very specific climates. Sugar beets, on the other hand, can be grown almost anywhere with far less water and **fertilizer**. They have made table sugar cheaper and widely available to more people.

**The period when humans
began to grow their
own food is called the
Agricultural Revolution.**

THE BIRTH OF FARMS

The Agricultural Revolution brought about
new technologies that made it easier for
humans to grow plants. Stone tools and
farming implements made it easier to work
the land, breed and domesticate plants,
and build better homes and farms.

ANCIENT FARMERS

For most of our history, humans were hunter-gatherers, chasing herds of large animals and collecting ripe fruits and vegetables as they moved from place to place. It was a simple but challenging life. Groups often consisted of families or small collections of families. Around 12,000 years ago, everything changed. People started to grow plants! This allowed them to settle down into larger groups, which became communities, which eventually became the cities we know today.

Many of the vegetables we eat today came from selecting and breeding different parts of wild cabbage—*Brassica oleracea*. From this one plant we got great new crops like broccoli, cabbage, kale, and cauliflower.

EVOLVING PLANTS

Evolution is a LONG process. Over thousands or millions of years, the plants, animals, and other organisms that are best at surviving in an **ecosystem** successfully reproduce, resulting in new generations that are even better adapted to survive. Humans figured out a long time ago that we could help that process along by choosing our favorite plants and planting their seeds. After doing that over and over again for thousands of years, we were able to create the fruits, vegetables, and plants that we know and love today!

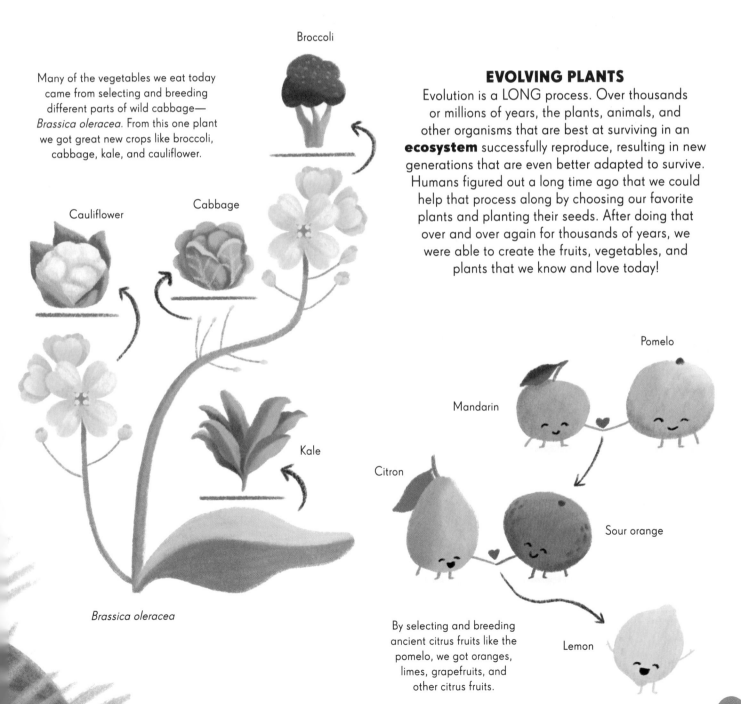

Broccoli

Cauliflower

Cabbage

Kale

Brassica oleracea

Pomelo

Mandarin

Citron

Sour orange

Lemon

By selecting and breeding ancient citrus fruits like the pomelo, we got oranges, limes, grapefruits, and other citrus fruits.

SAVE THE PRAIRIES!

Prairies are unique ecosystems made up mostly of grasses. They also contain a huge mix of flowers, shrubs, herbs, and other plants—though you normally won't see many trees. When we talk about ways to fight **climate change**, prairies often don't come into the conversation, but they're incredibly important. As prairie plants grow, die, and decompose year after year, they feed and shelter wildlife, take CO_2 out of the atmosphere, and add nutrients back into the ground. If we take care of them, these amazing ecosystems can help us save the world!

HOME ON THE PRAIRIE
Prairies are home to many different animals. It's common to find hundreds of different insects, rodents, birds, lizards, and even big mammals, such as bison and antelope. The rich diversity of plants provide food for the big animals—and plenty of places to live, hide, and hunt for the small ones!

Globally, prairies trap as much carbon and produce as much oxygen as trees.

Non-native prairie grass

Native prairie grass

NATIVE PLANTS
Native plants are those that naturally live in an area or country. They tend to be well suited to the environment and can grow and thrive with very little care, often sending roots farther down into the ground and producing bigger plants than non-native species.

MEDICINAL PLANTS
Many medicines we use today come from plants that live in the world's prairies. The grasses, wildflowers, and shrubs of these incredible places are extremely valuable to our health—from echinacea that boosts our immune systems and helps keep us from getting sick, to yarrow that helps treat wounds.

PRAIRIE-STYLE GARDENING
Although city landscapes are not natural, there are many things we can do to make them more environmentally friendly. Picking prairie plants that are well adapted to your climate means they require less watering and fertilizer. Plus, you don't need to use pesticides because the plants will attract bugs and birds that will take care of the pests for you!

IN PRAISE OF WOOD

Once upon a time, almost all our buildings were made with wood. Over time we started using more concrete and steel in construction, but in recent years wood is gaining in popularity again. Concrete and steel require **fossil fuels** to produce, leading to a lot of pollution. Wood can make the situation better! As trees grow, collect sunlight, and photosynthesize, they take CO_2 out of the atmosphere. This can then be locked away in the wood we build our homes with.

As trees are removed for their wood, new ones are planted in their place and the cycle can continue.

PLANTING RESPONSIBLY

Deforestation (cutting down trees irresponsibly) can harm the environment. It's important that forestry is performed in the correct way. As trees are cut down, new ones need to be planted. At the same time, studies must be conducted to make sure animals and ecosystems aren't harmed. If done correctly, forestry can be sustainable.

Most of the trees harvested for wood are grown on special plantations so we don't have to cut down old forests.

BY-PRODUCTS

Not much goes to waste in today's forestry industry. Wood that isn't used for construction is made into other useful things, from the page you're reading right now, to components in your phone, to mulch for gardens, and so much more!

LAMINATION STATION

New technology is making wood construction even better. Cross-laminated timbers are made by crisscrossing and gluing layers of wood together. They are as strong and fire-resistant as steel, while also more flexible and completely renewable.

WOODEN SKYSCRAPERS

Cities of the future may look a lot like cities of the past. New technologies in wood construction and ever-improving growing practices will continue to make wood a major material of choice. Imagine giant skyscrapers covered with plants and built from wood instead of concrete. What a wonderful, beautiful, ecologically conscious place that would be to live!

BAMBOO

Bamboo originally comes from Asia, where it has been used for thousands of years. Today, it's catching on as one of the most useful renewable resources in the world. It can be eaten, used to make clothes, replace wood in construction projects, and much more. Bamboo grows so fast, it's replenished almost as fast as it's used. Now that's a super plant!

PANDA SNACKS
Bamboo grows in the mountains of China where pandas live, and they can't get enough of it. In fact, it makes up more than 99% of their diet! This big, tough grass doesn't have a lot of nutrition in it, so pandas have to eat huge amounts every day.

BUILDINGS

Even though bamboo is more of a big grass than a tree, it can be used to make beautiful, strong buildings. Sometimes it's used in its natural pole form to make scaffolding or entire homes. Other times it's turned into boards and planks, which can then become walls or floors. It can be difficult to tell the difference between bamboo and wood.

FURNITURE

Bamboo is incredibly strong and, when heated, it can be very flexible too. It can be cut into strips, glued into bigger pieces, then turned into beautiful furniture that has little need for screws or nails. Imagine having a bamboo chair—the pandas would be jealous!

PILLOWS AND SOCKS

Move over, cotton and polyester, there's a new textile in town! Bamboo can be pulled apart into fibers, which are dried, bleached, and spun into strong and incredibly soft threads. Used for everything from pillows to socks, bamboo could be the sustainable fabric of the future.

EVERYDAY ITEMS

We use plastic to make things we use every day, from toothbrushes to combs. But amazingly bamboo can be used as a substitute for them all! Products made from this super plant can last a long time, and they will naturally break down (biodegrade) once they're thrown out, unlike plastic. This means they're better for the planet. Bamboo can even be used to make eco-friendly diapers for babies.

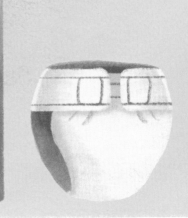

LIVING BRIDGES

Big, world-changing innovations don't have to be "new." In fact, many of the most amazing advances in science have been inspired by what nature and people in the past have already done. Living bridges are one such idea. By swapping steel and concrete for soil and branches, we could safely cross roads while helping the environment.

Living bridges would make cities cooler by reducing the amount of concrete heating up in the sun.

ANCIENT TREE BRIDGES

People in parts of India have been braiding together live tree branches and roots to make bridges for hundreds of years. These trees eventually grow together to cross rivers, streams, and ravines. In cities of the future, we may see a closer relationship between construction and plants. The same living bridges used in India for centuries could be grown to cross the spaces between skyscrapers!

ANIMAL CROSSING

Crossing busy roads is one of the most dangerous things an animal can do. Increasingly, large bridges planted with flowers, grass, and trees are being built over highways so wildlife can safely cross from one side to the other. People need to stay away from these wildlife bridges so they don't scare the animals.

GREENER CITIES

Life in the city can come with a lot of challenges, including heat, air pollution, water pollution, flooding, crime, poor health, poverty, and hunger. Problems such as these are common when you have lots of people living close together, driving cars, and building stuff out of concrete. Making cities greener can help solve these issues. Cities of the future could incorporate more plants to help clean the air and make lives better!

WORKING TOGETHER
Community gardens are public areas where people can grow their own fruits and vegetables. Studies have shown that community gardens lead to healthier populations, better eating habits, reduced crime, and an overall higher quality of life.

CITY OF THE FUTURE

Singapore, a small island nation in Southeast Asia, is a shining example of how we can make our cities greener. It's nearly impossible to tell where the plants stop and the buildings start! Green buildings have been mandatory since 2008 and giant "tree towers," rooftop gardens, and parks cover the landscape. Hopefully the future has more cities just like Singapore!

ROOFTOP GARDENS

Concrete rooftops in big cities are great places to build gardens. Popping up in more cities around the world, these gardens reduce heat, provide food, and offer places of calm for people living and working in tall buildings.

POLLINATOR HIGHWAY

Insects and other animals that pollinate plants are crucial to the health of our planet. As cities get bigger and wild spaces shrink, it's more difficult for these pollinators to navigate and find things to eat. By being thoughtful with how we design our cities and landscapes, we can help them survive!

FOLLOW THE GREEN ROAD

Towns and cities often lack green spaces. Plans for newer cities and developments include special "highways" of plants and parks that connect one green space to the next and make it easier for pollinators to get around. You can help this process by planting pollinator-friendly plants in your garden.

WHICH PLANTS ARE BEST?

Flowers are beautiful, but some are much better for pollinators than others. Local, or native, insects have developed close relationships with local plants over time. They are specially suited to collecting **pollen** and nectar from them. Wherever you live, you can find lists of wildflowers and native plants that will be perfect for your pollinator neighbors.

NATURE'S POWER

Most people know that spending time in nature is good for you. And now we're getting the science and data to back that up! Studies have shown that being around plants is good for your body and your brain. Whether you're sitting in a garden watching butterflies land on flowers or hiking through the woods, being with plants is guaranteed to make your day better.

FOREST BATHING

Forest bathing doesn't mean taking a bath out in the woods (though that would probably be nice). It just means spending time in forests. Scientists have discovered that walking through a park, sitting under a tree, or wandering through a forest can lower your blood pressure, reduce stress and anxiety, and drastically improve your mood. Some doctors even write prescriptions for forest bathing and taking nature walks!

CALMING TECHNIQUE

"Leaves on a stream" is a technique used by psychologists to help people deal with bad memories and stress. You envision your problems as leaves that are thrown into a stream. As the water carries the leaves away, you imagine it carrying your worries away.

HOSPITAL PLANTS

Have you or a family member ever had to spend time in hospital? It's no fun, so people often send flowers and plants to make us feel better. It turns out that's a great idea! Scientists have discovered that healing in patients is much faster when they have access to gardens in hospitals, can see plants from their hospital room, or have plants in the room with them.

GET WELL SOON

Though being in the forest is good for our mental health, spending time around plants can also help us heal faster and make us more physically fit. Scientists are still trying to figure out exactly why this happens, but it's becoming clear that we're so much healthier when plants are nearby. Doctors are using this knowledge to help their patients.

MEDICINAL BENEFITS

Plant-based remedies have been used all over the world for all of human history. Many of the medicines we have today were first discovered in different kinds of plants. Medicines made from plants can help us feel better and heal faster.

PLANT THERAPY

Working with plants and learning how to garden can help people stay fit, work through stress and trauma, overcome learning disabilities, and live happier lives. It's likely that a combination of improved mood, the oxygen provided by the plants, and maybe even chemicals released by the leaves of plants into the air have direct effects on our well-being.

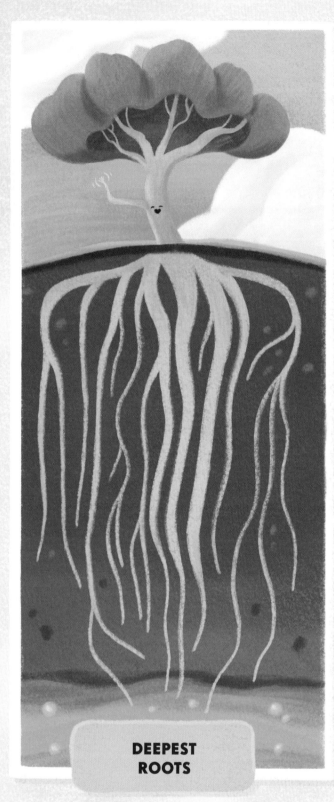

DEEPEST ROOTS

TOP OF THE CROPS

You should be well aware by now that plants absolutely rule, but some really stand out as the best of the best. These incredible plants push what is possible to the absolute limit—so I've decided to hand out some awards!

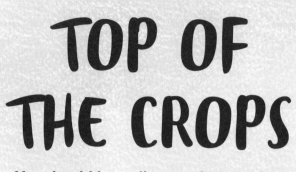

MOST OXYGEN

The shepherd's tree wins the award for deepest roots. Although these trees rarely grow more than 23 ft (7 m) tall, their roots have been found as far down as 246 ft (75 m)! Native to dry parts of Africa, these roots grow to such extreme depths looking for water.

All plants produce oxygen as they photosynthesize, but fir, spruce, beech, and maple trees are tied for the O_2 prize. Vast forests of these evergreen (fir and spruce) and deciduous (beech and maple) trees take carbon dioxide from the atmopshere and pump out oxygen for billions of humans and animals!

MOST USEFUL

MOST WIDELY EATEN

You already know our winner for the most useful prize: bamboo! Used for thousands of years to make everything from building materials to plates, bamboo is sustainable and 100% panda-approved.

Grown and consumed by billions of people all over the world, rice takes home the trophy for the most widely eaten plant on the planet. It grows in a number of different climates and can be used in all sorts of meals.

OLDEST PLANT

MOST NUTRITIOUS

Native to the western US, the bristlecone pine is the oldest plant in the world. The oldest one (that we know of) is named Methuselah. It's almost 4,800 years old!

A tree native to India called moringa is considered the most nutritious plant. It contains 92 different **nutrients** and 46 types of antioxidant, making it super healthy.

HONORABLE MENTIONS

STINKIEST

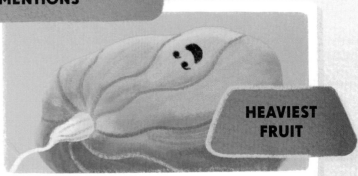

HEAVIEST FRUIT

The world's smelliest plant is the corpse flower. Standing at 12 ft (3.5 m) tall, it smells like rotting meat and is pollinated by flies. Stay clear!

Pumpkins are the heaviest fruits of them all. A man named Stefano Cutrupi once grew a pumpkin in Italy that weighed 2,303 lb (1,226 kg). Happy Halloween!

WHAT CAN YOU DO?

We've talked about all the ways plants can help save the world, but you can help too. There are so many ways we can all learn about amazing plants by growing them ourselves.

SMALL BUT MIGHTY

A lot of people think they have to have a large space to grow a garden, but that's the furthest thing from the truth! Window boxes are a great first place to grow plants, and you can check on them every time you look out the window.

Raised beds

CRAFTY GARDENING

If you're lucky enough to have some outdoor space, but no soil, you could grow plants in raised beds, pots, or containers. Ideally whatever container you use should have good drainage (holes in the bottom) because most plants don't like sitting in too much water.

MAKE IT A GROUP ACTIVITY

Gardening has been shown to make us healthier and happier, but it also brings us closer to one another. Growing plants is a perfect activity to do with your family or friends. It's a great way to unplug from our phones and tablets and spend some time together outside.

HOUSEPLANTS

Houseplants are a great way to get into gardening. From squishy succulents to prickly cacti, the plants we fill our homes with bring us a lot of joy and can teach us the basics of **horticulture**. Houseplants also help clean the air, give us more oxygen to breathe, and make our homes more beautiful.

HAS ANYONE SEEN MY BOOTS?

The truth is you can grow a garden pretty much anywhere. Anything that can hold a little bit of soil can be a perfect pot for your plants. An old boot? Sounds great! Some coffee jars and soup cans? You're good to go! The only limit is your imagination.

STARTING TO GROW

There are a lot of things you need to think about when starting to grow plants, but few are more important than light, water, and soil. Make sure the amount of light you have is correct for the plant you're trying to grow and that you have good access to a water source. Then get planting!

Growing plants you really like, from flowers to fruits and vegetables, is the key to keeping you excited about gardening. Here are some ideas for plants to start with.

Tomatoes like warm weather, lots of water and fertilizer, and plenty of light.

Chili peppers love heat and sunlight, and they can take a little drought.

Lettuces like a bit of shade and a good amount of water.

Grow your succulents in a bright spot. They don't need very much water!

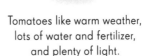

LOOKING TO THE FUTURE

We face a lot of challenges as we head into the future, but we're smart, brave, and have some great allies on our side: plants! We've learned of the amazing ways plants protect us, clean up the environment, and help make our world better. Scientists are working hard to find big solutions, but it's up to all of us to take charge of the way we interact with the environment. Let's find more ways to be more friendly to the wildlife around us. Let's love and appreciate nature wherever we find it. Let's be good to this planet that's so good to us.

Whether it's by planting native plants, recycling, composting, or learning more about the wondrous world of plant science, you (yes, YOU) can have a huge impact. We don't know what the future will look like, but wouldn't it be amazing if we kept finding new ways to mix cool technology with plants that have been doing their thing for millions of years? We all have the power and responsibility to make that happen. Plants are coming to the rescue, but we should keep doing our best to help them along the way so that everyone and everything on earth can enjoy clean air and a bright future!

GLOSSARY

Aeroponics
The process of growing plants in the air without soil. Similar to hydroponics, but nutrient-rich water is sprayed onto the plant roots instead of them being submerged in it.

Agriculture
The practice of farming, for example growing crops, breeding animals, and producing cotton and wool for clothing.

Algae
Tiny, plantlike organisms that live in water where they photosynthesise and produce much of the world's oxygen.

Breeding
Using the practice of pollination between two different plants to create a new variety of plant.

Carbon dioxide (CO$_2$)
A gas in our atmosphere that animals breathe out and plants absorb to use in photosynthesis. Too much CO$_2$ in the atmosphere can make climate change worse.

Chlorophyll
A green pigment plants use to capture energy from the sun for photosynthesis.

Climate change
Global warming and other long-term changes in the temperature and weather.

Composting
The process of turning organic matter, such as food scraps from your kitchen or leaves from your tree, into a fertilizer that can help plants grow.

Condensation
The process of water vapor (a type of gas) cooling and turning into a liquid. An example of this process is when clouds start to turn into rain.

Deforestation
The removal or destruction of trees from forests.

Ecosystem
A place where different living things (organisms) interact with one another and the environment.

Evaporation
The process of liquid water turning into a gas called water vapor.

Fertilizer
A rich source of nutrients that is used to help plants grow. Fertilizer can be bought or made by composting.

Fossil fuels
Fuels (energy sources) created over millions of years from the remains of living organisms. Examples include coal and oil.

Fungi
Organisms that live on and help to break down organic matter (like logs). Many fungi grow mushrooms to help them spread seedlike structures called spores, which is how they reproduce.

Genes
The material in all living cells that carries information that determines how a living thing will look and function.

Germination
The process of a seed growing into a plant.

Horticulture
The study of plants and gardens.

Hydroponics
The process of growing plants in nutrient-rich water without soil.

Insecticides
Chemicals used to kill insects that damage plants.

Microorganisms
Very, very small living things.

Mulch
Materials like bark, leaves, or compost that are spread around plants to make the soil healthier, save water by reducing evaporation, and help prevent weeds from growing.

Native species
A plant or animal that is originally from an ecosystem and is well adapted to living in it.

Non-native species
A plant or animal that lives in an ecosystem but originally came from a different ecosystem.

Nutrients
The different vitamins and minerals plants need to grow.

Organism
A living thing.

Oxygen (O₂)
A gas in our atmosphere released by plants that animals need to breathe to survive.

Photosynthesis
The process plants use to turn sunlight, water, and carbon dioxide into the sugars they need to grow.

Pollen
A powdery substance produced by plants that is used in the process of pollination to make fruit and seeds.

Pollination
The process of pollen being moved from one flower to another—often by insects—to make fruits and seeds.

Pollution
Substances released into the air by vehicles and buildings that cause harm to the environment.

Transpiration
The process of plants taking water out of the soil, using it, and then releasing it to the atmosphere as water vapor.

INDEX

This has been a

NEON SQUID

production

Author: Dr. Vikram Baliga
Illustrator: Brian Lambert
Editorial Assistant: Malu Rocha
US Editor: Allison Singer Kushnir
Proofreader: Joseph Barnes
Indexer: Elizabeth Wise

ABOUT THE AUTHOR

Dr. Vikram Baliga is a horticulture lecturer at Texas Tech University. He hosts the *Planthropology* podcast, where he interviews amazing people from the world of botany, and has a popular account on TikTok.

ABOUT THE ILLUSTRATOR

Brian Lambert creates art that is bright, vibrant, and versatile with a unique and warm-hearted feel. Brian enjoys working on illustrations from his home in the beautiful Inland Northwest. He spends his spare time drawing, dreaming, and hanging out with his wife and cat.